By the Same Author

Aerospace Power, *a Pictorial Guide*
Auto Racing
Be a Winner in Baseball
Be a Winner in Football
Be a Winner in Ice Hockey
Be a Winner in Tennis
Bicycling
Bush Flying in Alaska
Cleared for Takeoff, *Behind the Scenes at an Airport*
Deep-Sea World, *the Story of Oceanography*
Drag Racing
Motorcycling
Project Apollo, *Mission to the Moon*
Project Mercury
Rockets, Missiles, and Moons
Skyhooks, *the Story of Helicopters*
Skylab
Skyrocketing Into the Unknown
Spacetrack, *Watchdog of the Skies*

be a winner in BASKETBALL

BY CHARLES COOMBS

illustrated with 59 photographs
William Morrow and Company
New York   1975

Library of Congress Cataloging in Publication Data

Coombs, Charles Ira   (date)
  Be a winner in basketball.

  SUMMARY: Discusses the history and rules of basketball and gives hints on training, skills, and strategy.
    1. Basketball—Juvenile literature. [1. Basketball] I. Title.
GV885.1.C66   796.32′3   75-17778
ISBN 0-688-22039-8
ISBN 0-688-32039-2 lib. bdg.

ACKNOWLEDGMENTS FOR PHOTOGRAPHS
Carolina Cougars, pages 73, 79, 90; Denver Rockets, pages 13, 44, 72, 75, 85, 101, 109; Madison Square Garden Center, page 14; New York Nets, pages 10, 86; Philadelphia 76ers, pages 62, 76, 91, 96; Philadelphia Tigers, page 16; Phoenix Suns, pages 21, 46; Pierce College, page 23; San Antonio Spurs, page 64; United States Air Force Academy, page 29; Utah Stars, pages 18, 43, 105.
All other photographs were taken by the author.

contents

There is no more demanding and action-packed sport than basketball. Nor is any game more fun for players and spectators. Although the game is simple in concept —merely toss a ball through a hoop—the many skills it calls for are challenging to master. At garage-mounted hoops, school gymnasiums, and playground courts literally millions of young people—both boys and girls— spend countless hours sharpening the skills of the game.

There are many fine points in the techniques used by different players. Some are individual variations—"If it works it must be good." Some are coaches' preferences— "Your way is basically okay, but try this and see if it isn't better." (It usually is.)

In the process of research, I watched and listened to the "asphalt army" practicing uncoached fundamentals on roughly paved playground courts. I frequented high-school gyms on Friday nights, usually armed with cameras.

But it was at Pierce College, Woodland Hills, California, that I was most able to get a close-up view of players working on both individual and team skills. Not only did they display their talents on the hardwood, they willingly posed for many of the photographs in this book. Thanks to all of you.

Their coach, Larry Hankammer, patiently explained how things are done on the basketball court, and why. He also took time to read the manuscript and make suggestions.

Coach Tom Anderson, of University High School, in Los Angeles, also read the manuscript and added several helpful comments.

Having received such fine cooperation, I hope you will find that the information in this book is of value to your game. Now, go out and hit that hoop!

Charles "Chick" Coombs
Westlake Village, California
1975

More than any other sport, basketball is a game in which you must be able to do everything and at all times.

You may be a fine offensive player, a real deadeye when it comes to shooting baskets. But are you equally adept at defending your goal when your opponents have the ball and are threatening to score?

Can you pass, catch, dribble, cut, pivot, and jump? Can you use your left hand as well as your right? Are you quick? Do you have good judgment, so you can anticipate the direction in which a ball will ricochet off the backboard? Can you maneuver into the right spot and leap up in a tangle of groping hands and arms to grab a rebound?

If you are able to feint an opponent out of position, keep him from shooting, outwit him, outmaneuver him, and outrun him, as well as react immediately to sudden unplanned situations—a loose ball, an intercepted pass, a missed shot, an elbow in your ear—then you are a basketball player.

The exciting, high-speed, dazzling game of basket-

Shooting the corner shot is just one of the many skills
needed to play basketball.

ball demands that you be an all-around player. One-way
experts need not apply. Basketball is strictly a team
sport. If you wish to win, you have to think and practice
teamwork, teamwork, teamwork.

Nothing is more essential to basketball than running.

It is a running game. Forward, backward, and sideways. Good running requires quickness, balance, speed, and stamina. Running, like the many other skills necessary in basketball, is acquired mainly through learning fundamentals and practicing.

One sometimes wonders if Dr. James A. Naismith had any idea of what a challenging game he first put together back in 1891. At that time he was a physical-education teacher in the YMCA. He was looking for a game that could be played indoors during the cold winter months in Springfield, Massachusetts.

Since such sports as baseball, football, and soccer were popular, Dr. Naismith decided that his game— whatever it turned out to be—should use some kind of ball. He happened to have an old soccer ball handy, so he began with it.

He gathered some students around him and took the ball out on the gym floor. Dividing up sides, they tossed the ball around for a while but seemed to be getting nowhere in particular. Obviously there was no game in what they were doing. There was no real challenge, no goal to achieve.

No goal! That was it. They needed a goal. At first, Dr. Naismith considered putting a couple of boxes on each end of the floor and having the players bounce or shoot the ball into them. But no one was able to locate suitable boxes. The building's caretaker, however, did come up with a couple of tapered, round peach baskets that he found in a storeroom.

Resting on the floor, the baskets tipped over whenever a ball hit them. So Dr. Naismith decided to tack them to the facing of the balcony behind which was a second-story running track. He nailed a basket at each end of the court and soon discovered that the balcony facings made excellent backboards for banking the ball into the peach baskets. By chance, when the baskets were nailed in place, the rims were ten feet from the floor, which is the standard height to this day.

Each team, which at that time could be most any number of players, had to work the ball down the court and try to put it into the peach basket. A player was not allowed to carry or kick the ball but was supposed to move it by a series of passes.

Then someone got the clever notion that if he couldn't find any pass receivers in the clear, he'd simply pass to himself. So he dropped the ball a few feet in front of him, ran and grabbed it, bounced it again, chased it— and the dribble was born. Now there were two ways

Basketball is a contest
of chasing and being chased.

to move the ball around a basketball court—pass or
dribble.

In steady succession, other fine points of the game
were developed. The soccer ball gave way to a specially
designed basketball. Peach baskets were replaced with

Basketball has an enormous following of fans.

iron rings from which dangled woven nets of string. Regular backboards replaced the balcony facings for mounting the "baskets," which the rings are still called. Down through the years other developments turned the game into the action-filled and rhythmic contest it is today.

The popularity of basketball, the only major sport that has originated in the United States, has spread rapidly around the world. One reason is that YMCA workers took it with them when they went to work in foreign lands. By 1920, the game was being played in about fifty foreign countries, and in 1936 basketball became a regular event in the Olympic Games.

Basketball mania continued to grow. There simply was no game more challenging to play nor more fun to watch. High-school and college gyms overflowed with eager fans on game nights. Throughout the land most barns and garages sported basketball hoops, and still do. By the mid-1940's more people were playing basketball than any other sport, and more people were watching it.

Meanwhile, in order to help meet the needs of both those who wanted to play and those who preferred to watch, professional basketball teams came into being around the country. Often they played in dingy buildings normally used as dance halls, for Grange meetings, or some such thing. Sometimes teams had to carry their own backboards from town to town and mark off the court boundaries with tape. Even if there was a shower available for post-game freshening up, team members usually had to furnish their own soap and towels.

Although school leagues flourished, the pros continued to suffer from lack of organization and poor playing facilities. This situation began to change for the better in 1946 when the Basketball Association of America was formed. A few years later the BAA became the

National Basketball Association (NBA). Basketball at both school and professional levels had become well organized and remains so today.

The basic rules of basketball are fairly simple. There are five players on each team: two guards, two forwards, and a center, or pivot man. As a player, you may pass the ball in any direction with either or both hands. You may also bat it with your hands. Although you may not walk or run with the ball, you may move it around with

The dribble is a major skill in basketball.

a series of uninterrupted bounces, or dribbles. But once you stop your dribble, you cannot start again. You must get rid of the ball by passing it to a teammate or shooting it at the basket. A basket made during normal game action counts two points. A free throw awarded for an infraction of play and taken from the foul line counts one point.

In an effort to get the ball away from an opponent, you may not hold him, charge into him, trip him, or interfere with him in any way by bodily contact. Rules and good intentions notwithstanding, anyone who plays or watches basketball knows that considerable body banging takes place in this supposedly noncontact sport. Yet, if the contact is deliberate and overly energetic, the referee's whistle will shrill and a penalty will be assessed.

Still, you must try to get the ball away from an opponent. You should block his path, slow him down, guard and harass him so he cannot make a decent pass or get a clear shot at the basket.

These are the simple basics of the game. And the simplest of all is that the team able to put the ball through the basket the most times during the playing period wins the game. Obviously, therefore, shooting is most important. However, it is no more important than the strategy and skill required of all members of a team to work the ball down the court and get it to a player in the clear and close enough to the basket so he has a better than average chance of putting it through the hoop. This is known as high-percentage shooting and is a key to most victories.

Putting the ball through the hoop
is what the game is all about.

When basketball began, no one gave much thought to a player's height. A quick player was as good as a tall player; in fact, perhaps a little better, for often he could move himself and the ball with more dexterity. Most shots at the basket were then two-handed, and underhand at that. The shot began at about the level of the knees. A defender didn't have to be tall to block such shots effectively.

Then, since the basket hangs ten feet from the floor, players began to seek the shortest route between two points. They started to shoot their shots overhand. But they still used two hands on the ball. Thus began the chest-high two-hand shot, which enabled the taller players to launch the ball quickly and beyond the reach of many shorter players. It was a good shot and is still used occasionally.

However, other developments soon took place. Instead of using two hands on the ball, a few players began to launch the sphere toward the basket with one hand in a style similar to that of shot-putting. With practice, accuracy improved, and the shot came to be known as the one-hand push shot, or one-hand set shot. Although its popularity began in the West, the one-hand shot soon became universal, thus putting a premium on tall players; the taller the player the better chance he had of batting down a push shot.

What followed next? Well, one way to get the shot up and over the outstretched hand of perhaps a taller player was to jump straight up in the air a foot or so and launch the ball toward the hoop while at the peak of the leap. The technique worked beautifully—after much practice—and the highly popular and very effective one-hand jump shot came into being.

Pretty much the same sort of thing was happening to the pass. As players became taller and taller, more and more passes were thrown overhead to high-reaching hands—anything to keep the ball above the reach of the shorter opponents.

So, to a considerable degree, basketball has become a tall man's game. The tall man has the advantage of outreaching his opponent, probably of outjumping him, and of grabbing the rebound, all of which are important considerations in basketball.

But can a tall man outrun a shorter man? Can he outshoot him? Can he outthink him? Is he any more aggressive? Does he have better stamina? Does he have any stronger desire to win?

The answer, in a word, is no. Height has little ad-

Opposite: The one-hand jump shot is basketball's finest weapon.

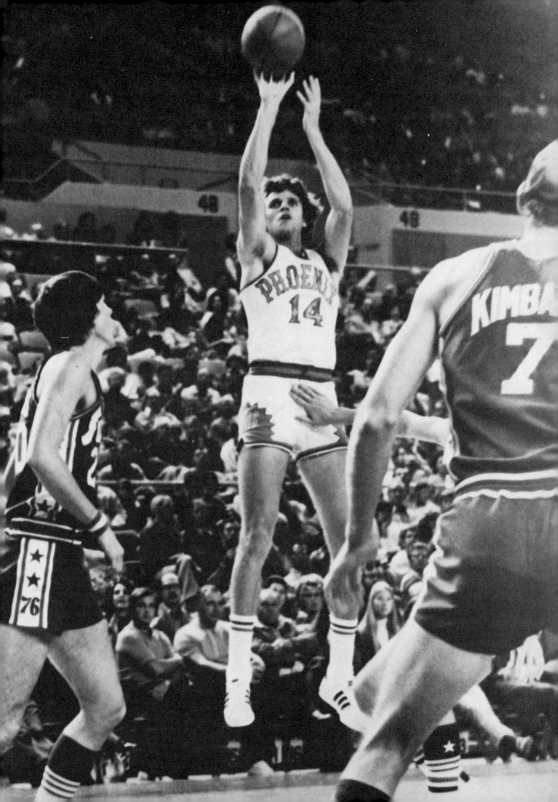

vantage other than reach, so there is as much place in basketball for the shorter man as there is for the "skyscraper." Few teams are without at least two shorter, quicker, more aggressive "take-charge" guys. Usually they play the guard positions. They move fast, handle the ball skillfully with either hand, bark out signals, sparkplug plays, dribble, pass, and weave. They befuddle the opposition and, indeed, take and make their full share of shots. Generally speaking, the shorter player is able to do more things well, and this versatility easily makes up for whatever he may lack in height and reach.

Almost from the beginnings of the game, girls have also played basketball. Women's basketball is included in most school athletic programs, and it has moved into the field of professional sports too. Though there are often minor differences in rules between boys' and girls' basketball, by and large, girls' teams now play the same game as the boys, based on the same fundamentals of passing, dribbling, running, guarding, faking, shooting, and footwork.

Paraplegics and other handicapped people unable to use their legs play basketball in wheelchairs. They even

Girls' basketball is played with basically similar rules
as boys' basketball and demands equal skills.

have regular competitive conferences. They play a
spirited and skillful hoop game, despite frequent col-
lisions and occasional topplings of wheelchairs.

23

Indeed, basketball is for anyone and everyone who is interested. You start out, of course, by wanting to play and believing that you can. In other words, you have enthusiasm and self-confidence. With both, you are halfway to your goal.

The other half is acquiring the fundamentals of the game. Begin by learning them correctly and thus avoid developing bad habits that are difficult to get rid of. Read a little to learn what is expected of you and what your responsibilities are.

Start by going through the motions, with or without a basketball or a basket. If necessary, you can practice alone, but for more fun and better practice buddy up with one or more of your friends so you can work competitively. Your skills will develop more quickly if you set up one-on-one, two-on-two, or some such form of rivalry that at least somewhat resembles game conditions.

And then, above all, pay attention to good coaching. An experienced coach will quickly spot flaws in your game. He will offer suggestions for correcting them. Start right, and stay right.

You may be short or tall, thin or thick. Your size and shape are not as important as your desire to play. You may not be fast, but you can make up for that lack by being aggressive and quick. Your shooting eye may be off. Practice until it's on target. Then keep on practicing. And learn those fundamentals.

From the public playground to Madison Square Garden, from Iowa to Istanbul, basketball is a universal game. If you really came to play, you'll get your chance.

One-on-one rivalry makes basketball
a testing ground of offensive and defensive skills.

chapter two
READY TO PLAY

In order to become skilled at basketball, you need a suitable place to play and proper equipment. A springy wood or composition indoor court, with standard dimensions, is nice to play on. But you can't always rely on finding one. Many a high-school, college, or professional superstar has practiced uncounted hours on the

Playground basketball is a national pastime.

slanted, cracked concrete driveway in front of the family garage, on the rough asphalt of a playground, or even on slippery farmyard dirt. A place is almost always available, if you really want to practice.

It's far better, of course, if you can play on an approved court, with and against teammates and opponents having similar talents. From such informal practice sessions and make-up games, you develop the skills that lead to victories in organized play.

The standard basketball court for college and professional games is 94 feet long by 50 feet wide. Those are the inside dimensions, since the boundary lines themselves are considered out-of-bounds. The ideal high-school court is the same width, but 10 feet shorter than a college court.

Often, however, the boundaries of a basketball court must be measured according to the space available in the gymnasium, auditorium, outdoor area, or wherever the playing surface happens to be. Though not ideal, such variations from the norm should have no discouraging effect on your game. If you really want to play basketball, you will find a way to do so in the space available.

Most favored basketball courts have a hardwood surface. These surfaces provide a little spring, or give, and absorb some of the pounding and jarring of constant running. A wooden floor also is solid enough to provide a lively bounce to the ball. Occasionally courts have a thin synthetic surfacing made of rubber and resin compounds similar to those used for other sports. But probably more basketball games are played on park and school-ground asphalt than any other place, simply because these facilities are more available to the young player.

Regardless of size or surfacing, an approved basketball court is divided across the middle by a center line that separates the playing surface into a team's backcourt (defensive) and front court (offensive). This dividing center line is commonly called the ten-second line, which is the maximum amount of time a team in possession of the ball is allowed to move the ball from its backcourt across that line to its front court.

In the exact middle of the court is a center circle 4 feet in diameter. This circle is used for jump balls, or center tips, which begin each quarter or half, as well as play after certain interruptions such as held balls or double fouls. Around the 4-foot circle is a 12-foot circle called the "restraining ring." All players other than the two jumpers must remain outside this restraining ring during the center tip.

Protruding in from each end of the court is a rectangular key, also known as the free-throw, or foul, lane. The key is 19 feet long, extending from the end line to the free-throw line, which is 15 feet from the basket itself. On school courts the lane is 12 feet wide; on professional courts it is 16 feet wide. The lane is there to keep players from crowding under the basket during free throws or during the game action itself.

While play is under way, members of the offensive team are not allowed to occupy that lane for more than

Resilient composition or hardwood surfaces make the best courts.

three seconds at a time. This time limit relieves possible congestion under the basket and keeps the game under control. Since most professional players are big, rough, and powerfully aggressive, they have wider restrictive lanes.

Each free-throw line is enclosed within a circle 12 feet in diameter, the same size as the center restraining ring. Its purpose is to keep other players away during jump balls at the foul line following a call for held ball.

Except for a few small lane-space marks by which players from opposing teams are kept separated as they line up for rebounds of missed free throws, these are the major court markings.

On courts used in American Basketball Association professional games a long-shot zone is added. Actually, this zone includes all the area that lies outside a line that runs parallel to and 3 feet from each sideline, then curves outward beyond the key to a distance of 25 feet from the backboard. In ABA competition, field goals made from outside the line count three points rather than the normal two.

The most important item of court makeup is the basket, or goal, set 4 feet in from each end line. Actually the front surface of the backboard is 4 feet from the

Opposite: Standard basketball court diagram

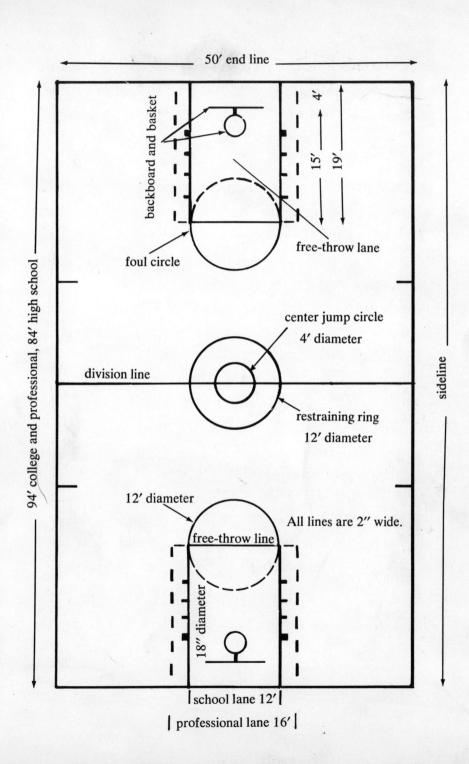

50' end line

backboard and basket

4'

15'

19'

free-throw lane

foul circle

center jump circle
4' diameter

division line

restraining ring
12' diameter

94' college and professional, 84' high school

sideline

12' diameter

All lines are 2" wide.

free-throw line

18" diameter

school lane 12'

professional lane 16'

Hoop and backboard

end line. This backboard usually is a rectangle 4 feet high by 6 feet wide. Many high schools and playgrounds, however, use fan-shaped backboards, which are somewhat smaller (54 inches wide) but fully effective.

Backboards are often made of wood or composition. Some boards are made of glass or other transparent material so that end-zone spectators can watch the ball all the way to the hoop. Transparent backboards have a rectangle 18 inches high by 24 inches wide outlined on the glass above the basket to define the target area for the shooter.

32

The hoop, or basket, is a metal ring with an 18-inch inner diameter. The ring is securely attached to the backboard at an equal distance from each vertical edge. The top of the hoop is parallel to and 10 feet from the floor.

The ring is suspended at a distance of 6 inches out from the backboard on a bracket, usually welded to the ring itself. Dangling about 18 inches down from the ring is a tapered string net, somewhat funnel-shaped.

Basketball is a running game.

Not only does this net aid the shooter's aim, it eliminates any doubt about whether the ball actually went through the hoop.

Early-day basketballs were somewhat larger than the present streamlined, easy-to-handle versions. Originally they were made of leather wrapped around an inflatable rubber bladder, and they were not always perfectly round. Today's basketball is more likely to be a multi-layered sphere of rubber compounds and nylon windings covered with a thin skin of leather or material that is pebble-grained to resemble leather. It is considerably more durable and true to shape than the old ball. Most basketballs are a russet brown color. However, ABA pros use a red-white-and-blue striped ball.

An official basketball must be between $29\frac{1}{2}$ and 30 inches around, and it should weigh betwen 20 and 22 ounces. It is properly inflated to between $7\frac{1}{2}$ and $8\frac{1}{2}$ pounds per square inch of pressure, so that when dropped from a height of 6 feet onto a hardwood floor, it will bounce back up between 49 and 54 inches.

Most of all, insofar as you are concerned, the ball should have "eyes" for finding its way through the hoop.

Some games can be run by a single official, although it is better to have two, a referee and an umpire. A school conference or professional basketball game is such a fast and furious contest that usually two officials are required to keep up with the infractions of rules and to see that the competition doesn't get out of hand. Often they are assisted by a timer and a scorer. Of course, in playground make-up games you usually have to do your own officiating, but there's no reason for a lot of arguments, since you're playing for fun.

Game times vary considerably. The very young often play six-minute quarters, with suitable intermissions in between. High schoolers play eight-minute quarters. College teams divide their games into two twenty-minute halves, with about a fifteen-minute rest period in between.

On the other hand, the pros divide their game into quarters of twelve minutes each, with a minute and a half intermission between quarters and about fifteen minutes between halves.

Tie games are usually decided by a short overtime period, or more than one if necessary.

To be a basketball player, you must be in top physical condition. There is really no more demanding game in all of sports than basketball. Whether or not you have

the ball, you are continually moving or should be. On offense, it is important that you decoy players away from the ball handler so that he can set up to shoot. And you must be able to pursue the man you are supposed to be guarding tirelessly or constantly hound and harass an opposing player who has possession of the ball.

You are not born with speed and strength. You gain strength by exercising. You gain speed by running, and running some more. Both add up to stamina.

In order to earn your position on a team, get into top physical condition before the season begins. Start ahead of time during the summer months.

Good footwork also is essential in basketball. You're on your feet constantly—running, pivoting, stopping, starting, leaping, and jumping. Exercise will toughen your feet so they can withstand the steady twisting and pounding they will be subjected to. Strengthen your ankles by doing stretching and turning exercises, but do them carefully and regularly. Bending over until you touch the floor is good for stretching the leg muscles and preventing hamstring injuries.

You can also try lifting weights. Of course, this exercise will benefit your entire body, not just your feet, ankles, and legs. Do your weight lifting on a programed

Opposite, top: Stretching limbers you up for a game.
Bottom: Practice spread-eagle jumps for skill in rebounding.

basis, starting at about twenty pounds and increasing the weight. But don't overdo the lifting; bulging muscles are not nearly as important as loose, well-conditioned muscles.

You should try to strengthen your hands and wrists. Most any sensible exercise, such as squeezing an old rubber ball, fingertip push-ups, or isometrics as, for example, pushing your fingers hard against an unyielding wall, will strengthen your fingers and hands, wrists and arms.

Do calisthenics—body bends, simulated bicycle pedaling. Stretch and stretch some more. Basketball demands fast reactions. You will constantly be spinning in your tracks, pivoting, and reversing direction. Unless your muscles are kept stretched and flexible, you stand a chance of straining a muscle or pulling a ligament.

Wear good shoes, properly soled and supported in the arch. Be sure they're the correct size. Tight shoes restrict circulation and cause exhausting discomfort. On the other hand, if your shoes are so large that your feet slide around inside of them, you will certainly be plagued with blisters. Lace your shoes snugly, but not too tightly. Sometimes a pair of cotton socks under your sweat socks will add comfort and help prevent blisters

Wear high or low tops, whichever you prefer,
but do a better job of lacing than shown here on right.

in case your shoes are a little large. Wearing high tops
or low tops is strictly a matter of preference.

Before a game try to get a good night's sleep. Sufficient rest will give you added stamina during the contest.

Pay attention to your diet. Go easy on the fats and
sweets, and load up on energy-producing protein. Fruit
juice, cereal, eggs, and lean meat make a good break-
fast or lunch. And lunch is the last meal you should eat
before an afternoon game. Before a night game you can
have a light dinner, but restrict it to proteins. In no
case, however, should you eat later than three full hours

before a game. A full or even partially full stomach will bog you down and may make you ill during the heat of battle.

In other words, you should live sensibly, eat well-balanced meals, and get plenty of exercise. You'll know when you feel right.

Then it's high time to start testing your strength and endurance by getting out on a basketball court and playing with your friends. Do your turning, your cutting, your sidestepping, and reversing. Sprint and stop. Dribble and pivot and shoot. Be an actor. Fake and feint. Try to fool your opponents. Coordinate your movements. Keep your body in balance. Put rhythm in your moves.

Run and keep running.

Think basketball.

chapter three
MOVING THE BALL

Nothing happens in basketball unless you make it happen, and you do that by moving the ball around. Never let it rest. Don't be caught standing still.

There are two basic ways to move the ball up and down a basketball court. One is to dribble; the other is to pass. Usually a combination of the two is used. Of course, catching passes also is important. So actually you are using three fundamental skills for moving the ball—dribbling, passing, and catching.

To get possession of the ball, usually you will catch a pass, force a turnover, or grab a rebound off the backboards. In any case, possession is likely to occur during some fast action on the court. When you get hold of the ball, you may take no more than two steps before you must come to a stop or get rid of it. This two-count rhythm is all important, since game rules prohibit carrying the ball. Left foot, right foot (or vice versa), then stop.

While holding the ball, you may use either foot as a pivot foot. Keeping this foot in contact with the floor, you may swing around with the other foot as much as you want. But if you move or lift your pivot foot before getting rid of the ball, you will be called for traveling, and the ball goes over to the other team. So, once you get the ball, learn to come to a quick stop, with your feet planted in the most effective position from which to pivot, pass, or dribble.

When dribbling, you move the basketball around the court with a series of controlled bounces. You may dribble while standing still or while moving rapidly. You lean your body a little forward in a relaxed position, with your knees bent in a slight crouch. Keep your head up and your eyes forward; this is one time in sports when you don't watch the ball. As your eyes scan the action, you dribble by feel.

The difficulty comes when, while still dribbling, you have to weave and dodge around the floor, spinning away from clutching hands and avoiding churning, defensive action. Since the ball is in and out of your possession as you bounce it, you need a great deal of skill, confidence, and poise to maintain control of it.

To be a good dribbler, you must practice using either hand until you are able to switch from side to side automatically. You do the dribbling itself with an easy pumping motion of your forearm, wrist, and fingers. Stay relaxed. Don't simply slap the ball to the floor. Push it down rhythmically, keeping your fingertips in contact with it as long as possible. Remember, use the pads of your fingertips more than the palm of your hand.

In dribbling, know where the ball is without looking at it.

Ride the ball up and down with your hand,
maintaining contact as long as possible.

This sensitive touch enables you to control the direction,
height, and speed of your dribble.

As the ball hits the floor and bounces back, your
fingertips are right there to ride back up with it. Thus,
the ball is never far from your dribbling hand and al-

ways under control. In most cases, you will find yourself dribbling through and around traffic, which calls for handling the ball low, using snappy bounces and keeping it in close to you for protection. So you crouch low over the ball, head up, and eyes forward. Bounce the ball no more than twelve to eighteen inches, for the lower the bounce, the better control you have over it. Shorter players usually make the best dribblers.

Behind-the-back dribbling is usually considered "showboating," but at times comes in handy for a skilled performer.

However, if you are trying to cover a lot of distance in a hurry and are not impeded by opposing players, you may straighten up more and bounce your dribble high and well out in front of you. Just don't dribble so far out in front that you can't catch up to the ball. If you let it bounce so high that you have to reach up and turn it over to bring it down, you will be called for traveling, or palming, and the ball goes to your opponents.

A dribble must be a continuous series of bounces. Once you interrupt the action or put two hands on the

When dribbling, keep the ball as far from
your opponent's reach as possible.

ball, you cannot start another dribble. You must pass the ball off or shoot.

When dribbling, try to keep your body between the ball and any opponent trying to get his hands on it. If someone charges toward you from the right, you must shift the ball to your left hand, away from him. If you are unable to do so, you should get rid of the ball quickly or an opponent can easily slap it away or steal it from you.

Don't let your free arm simply dangle at your side as you dribble. Keep it up in front of you or off to the side. Not only can your arm be used to ward off attacks, it can be ready to recover a ball that gets out of control. It also should be ready to take over the dribble when you decide to change hands.

You may even learn to dribble behind your back or between your legs. But do this fancy stuff sparingly, and only after you have practiced it to a point of perfection. Above all, don't use it for the sake of showing off, or showboating, but only when such deception will help your team to win.

Dribbling comes in handy when you're closely guarded. Dribble when you drive toward the basket for a lay-up. Dribble on a fast break when your teammates are covered. Dribble sometimes to draw a foul on a player who is swarming all over you. And dribble sometimes to move the ball around and open up the game.

But since dribbling is not as fast or effective as passing, you should never dribble when you can pass. In fact, passing is so important to winning basketball games that it is considered second in importance only to shooting. Most coaches have their teams put at least as much practice time and effort into their passing game as into their shooting game.

There is a wide assortment of passes at your disposal. The situation on the court at any given moment determines which pass you should use to be most effective. Some of the major passes are:

Two-hand chest. Also called a push pass, it is one of the most commonly used in basketball. It is particularly effective as a team gets close in to its basket, but is useful anywhere on the court.

In executing the chest pass, grip the ball with the fingers and thumbs of both hands, protecting it by keeping it close to your body. Have your thumbs behind the ball, with your fingers gripping it toward each side. Flex your knees and face your target.

48

In the two-hand chest, or push, pass
snap the ball out and follow through.

You start the pass with a sort of looping motion as
you bring the ball toward your chest. Without hesi-
tating, you step toward your receiver. Uncock your
wrists to add thrust, and snap the ball outward, guiding
it with your fingers and thumbs.

Pass briskly toward your target and follow through,

The overhead pass . . . and follow-through

turning your palms out, thumbs down, and fingers point-ing at the target. Use this pass a lot, particularly at short to medium range. It's a winner.

Overhead. This pass is the one used most in basket-ball. You start in a manner similar to the two-hand chest pass. Where traffic is thick, the best way to get the ball to a teammate is over the congestion, not through it. Gripping the ball with your fingertips, you raise it up over your head, rotating the fingers back a little as you bend and cock your wrists.

Now step toward your target, uncocking your wrists, and snap the ball off your fingertips. Your follow-through is abbreviated as you rotate your wrists with hands downward and outward. This is primarily a wrist pass. Use only what arm motion you need to add accuracy, velocity, and distance to the pass.

The over-the-shoulder, or baseball, pass is used for distance.

The overhead pass is used frequently for getting the ball to the pivot man as he maneuvers around the key, or foul circle, to receive the ball and lay up a shot to the basket. The overhead pass also is used frequently by the pivot man to clear the ball away from his position around the key.

Over-the-shoulder. This pass is similar to throwing a baseball; in fact, it often is called the baseball pass. Because of the basketball's larger size, however, keep both hands on it as you bring it back behind your ear. Then, as you draw it farther back, release the holding hand and keep the throwing hand directly behind the ball.

Point your free hand toward your target, which is probably an imaginary spot toward which a teammate is racing, step forward, and throw the ball overhand and past your ear. Use your body, legs, shoulders, and arms in the pass. Push off with your right foot, and shift your weight onto your forward swinging left foot as your arm comes through. It's the same natural movement used in baseball. (Directions in this book apply to right-handed players. If you're left-handed, simply reverse the procedure.)

The over-the-shoulder pass usually is used for long-range and sometimes full-court passes in order to get

Sometimes you can feed the ball to a teammate
with a short underhand pass, or hand-off.

the ball to a player streaking down the floor on a fast
break. It requires a good arm and a good eye, and it is
always risky. But, used properly, it often picks up extra
baskets.

Underhand. Since the main idea when moving a basketball around is to keep it up high, this pass is used
sparingly. The underhand pass is more of a hand-off
than an actual pass. If you try winding up to make an
underhand pass with either or both hands, the defense
can see it coming and will move to block it. So you use

underhand passes only in close quarters, perhaps on a give-and-go play where the pivot man simply thrusts the ball out for you to take off the palm of his outstretched hand as you streak past toward the basket.

Bounce. Sometimes, due to good guarding on the part of your opponents, there may be no safe aerial route for passing to a teammate. Here a bounce pass may come in handy. You usually start it from a low chest-pass position, say below chest level, since a major reason for using a bounce pass is to keep the ball under out-reaching hands.

Move the ball over medium to short distances with a bounce pass.

A bounce pass is a slowed pass, due to the friction of the bounce, and should be used over medium to short distances only. As you snap the ball forward, using both hands, aim for a spot on the floor about two thirds of the way to your receiver. Put some zip on the ball, but leave out the spin. A spinning ball not only takes a lop-sided bounce, it is difficult to handle. The time to cross a team up with bounce passes is when the defenders are leaping and jumping in anticipation of knocking down aerial passes. Sometimes you may use a one-hand push pass to bounce the ball down and around the reach of an opponent.

These passes are the primary ones used in basketball, but they certainly do not make up the entire inventory. There are hook passes, jump passes, behind-the-back passes (which fool the receivers as often as they fool the opposition, however), and even a pass that you roll along the floor (to be used sparingly in emergency situations when there is no other way to get the ball to a teammate). The secret of good passing is to know which pass to use in each situation. Any pass that will get the ball to a teammate in the right place at the right time is a good pass.

Be wary of using cross-court passes or high-lob passes. Either one is easy to intercept for a costly turnover to the other team.

No pass can be considered successful unless it is caught, which makes the receiver essential also. As a receiver, you seldom will be able to stand still and wait for the pass to come your way. First you will need to shake yourself free from whoever is trying to guard you. Doing so may take a great amount of pivoting, feinting, faking, and "playing without the ball," which is considered the most important part of an offense.

Yet, somewhere along the line, the pass will arrive where you are supposed to be. You must reach out for it, get it, and hold onto it, or the whole play goes down the drain.

An important rule in all ball handling is to control the ball with your fingers and thumbs. Don't try to hold it in the palms of your hands. If possible, use two hands to catch a pass. Catch a high pass with your fingers up and thumbs together. Catch low passes with fingers pointed down and little fingers next to each other.

However, more often than not, you are moving and the ball is coming at you from some angle. Reach out and block the ball with whichever hand is farthest from

Left: Catch a high pass with fingers up.
Right: Catch a low pass with fingers pointed down.

the passer, and secure it with the other hand. When done quickly and skillfully, this commonly used method of pass catching can hardly be discerned from a two-hand catch and is equally effective.

Always keep your eyes on the ball as it approaches. Step toward it and reach out. Keep your hands firm enough to stop the ball, yet relaxed enough to absorb

57

the shock of contact and prevent the ball from bouncing off fingers or palm. Quickly bring the ball in toward the protection of your body. Hold it about waist-high, from which position you are instantly prepared to move—dribbling, shooting, or passing off again, whatever the situation calls for.

Of course, you will not always be able to plan your method of catching a pass. Plenty of times you will have to grab the ball any way you can. You will stretch out, stab for it, try in whatever desperate manner to knock it down and get control of the evasive sphere. Sheer scrambling, too, comes under the heading of ball handling, which is largely what basketball is all about.

Basketball begins and ends with shooting. Regardless of how well you perform your other important functions in the game, you have not mastered the heart of basketball unless you can shoot.

At one time teams had shooting specialists. Usually they were the center and forwards, who played closest to the basket. Only occasionally did guards shoot, and they were often the low scorers. But in today's speeded-up, all-court type of basketball, in which players weave around and change positions constantly, every player must be able to shoot well. Guards, in fact, are often the high scorers. Playing this kind of balanced basketball is the only way to win.

There are certain important fundamentals to keep in mind when shooting. You must work on your concentration as avidly as you do on the proper release of the ball. Shooting usually is done during the most exciting and confusing times of a game. Unless you can erase the shouting and stomping and outreaching hands from your ears, eyes, and mind, you will not be able to decide which shot to use or give it the relaxed touch so necessary to accuracy. Despite the fierce activity surrounding you, you must learn to adjust the ball in your hands, take your sighting on the basket, and release your shot before the confusion and clutching hands close in on you.

You should practice all types of shots and from various distances. In time, you will sense which shot to use from different floor positions. Without limiting yourself to any particular shot, you will get an idea of which ones are your best percentage shots, those most likely to score points. Naturally they are the ones you should use most often. If you are unable to get into a good position to use your better shots, pass to a teammate rather than force a low percentage shot.

Put a normal amount of spin on the ball, but shoot it softly, with a gentle arch. In this way you give the ball a chance to bounce in off the rim if you miss a clean swisher. A twirling or a hard-thrown ball is more apt to spin or ricochet away.

Often players and coaches disagree as to whether to aim the ball directly for the hoop or to bank it off the backboard and through the basket. In general, on angle shots the more effective technique is to aim for a spot

60

on the backboard and bank the ball through the hoop. For straight-in shots, or shots from the corners, you should aim just over the rim of the basket itself. If it's late in the game and you are tiring, you may do better to aim for the back rim, thus allowing for the slightly shorter flight a tired shot may make. These decisions will come more easily after much practice and experience.

Actually, some top-notch players disdain using the backboard practically all of the time, and do very well indeed. However, it is there to use and, in most cases, can be used to good advantage.

Positioning the ball in your hands should be automatic. You will hold the ball in different ways depending upon the type of shot you are taking. You adjust your fingers across the seams in whatever way you have found most comfortable and sure. You should not have to look at the ball, because your eyes should be centered on your target—the basket. The sooner you lock your vision onto the basket, the more time your mental computer will have to judge distances and playing conditions and pass the word on to your muscles.

Usually as you prepare to take a shot, you must keep the ball close to you and reasonably high for protection. Keep your elbows in and low, cocked and ready to un-

coil. Propel the ball with a smooth upward unbending of the elbow, a snap of the wrist, then release it off your fingertips. Your shot may begin with the ball resting against the palm or pads of your hand, but your fingertips give it the final guidance.

Practice shooting with someone guarding you. Not that shooting by yourself isn't beneficial, but a harassing defender forces you to concentrate and maneuver into a prime position before attempting a shot. This one-on-one exercise is strenuous fun and practice at its best.

The following are some of the most frequently used shots:

Lay-up. This close-in shot sometimes begins with receiving a pass or, more often, with a dribble. It is considered to be the easiest shot in basketball and is the first one that you should learn to make.

To make a lay-up, drive in toward the basket, preferably from about a forty-five-degree angle, on either side. Just as you should be able to dribble skillfully with either hand, you should be able to make the lay-up approaching from either side or from straight ahead, using either hand.

Perhaps you fake your man out of position, pivot

Opposite: Driving in for a left-handed lay-up

around him, and dribble in from the right. Keep your dribble low and away from him until you are in the open. Now, as you approach the basket, dribble higher, and make the final bounce highest of all. Thus, you have already straightened up and without having to reach down for it, the ball comes into your hands. Glue your eyes on the mental bull's-eye you have chosen on the backboard, and take off.

You should take off about five or so feet out from

For a lay-up, get as high up
to the basket as you can.

the basket, since you want to jump high rather than far. Approaching from the right, take off on your left foot, lifting the ball high overhead with both hands. At the peak of your jump, take the left hand away from the ball and let the fingers of your shooting hand loft the ball easily against the backboard. Put the ball up without spin, so that it caroms gently down through the hoop.

Some players lift the ball upward with their shooting hand underneath it. Others lay it toward the basket in an overhand position, with fingers up and palm facing the backboard. Do what is comfortable and what is demanded by the action going on around you. The fingers-up position gets the ball higher more quickly. However, one advantage of the underhand action is that your body automatically twists around as you lay the ball up. When you come down, you are facing the court, ready to head back on defense if you make the basket or to get the rebound if you miss. Both methods have merits. Always shoot with your left hand when coming in from the left side, and vice versa on the right side. Thus, as you go up, your body is between the ball and the man guarding you.

Practice lay-ups. They are basic to good basketball.

Two-hand chest. This type of shot is what basketball was based on years ago. If you couldn't work the ball in for a lay-up, you stayed outside and heaved it goalward with both hands.

However, though the two-hand shot has given way to the one-hand, it is still a worthy weapon in a basketball player's arsenal. Most beginning young players need and use it until they are strong enough to propel the ball up to the basket with one hand.

In executing the two-hand chest shot, hold the ball lightly between both hands. Spread your fingers on the sides of the ball with your thumbs pointing toward each other behind the ball. Keeping elbows in, bring the ball up so you can sight over it at the basket. Position your feet comfortably apart, and bend a little at the knees. As you shoot, bring the ball toward you in a short looping motion. Straighten your knees as you rotate your arms upward and release the ball. On the release, turn your hands outward and follow through with arms fully extended as the ball arches toward the basket.

Although infrequently used, the two-hand chest shot is often good at a distance. It is used many times by players of the American Basketball Association when trying a three-point shot from the long-shot zone. Normally twenty feet is a reasonable outer limit for properly controlled basketball shots. Anything beyond is a sort of pump-and-pray proposition. A few pros still practice the two-hand chest shot for those beat-the-buzzer, last-second rafter rattlers. It can, of course, be used whenever and wherever there is time to pull up and take aim.

One-hand set, or push. You try to brake to a stop after a dribble or after receiving a pass and make this shot from a set position. Just as with the two-hand shot, you plant your feet and bend your knees. With both hands you bring the ball smoothly down and back toward you in a looping motion. Then, as it arrives about chest-high, you straighten your knees and start the upward flow of motion.

Now the technique changes from that of the two-hand shot. You bring the pushing hand behind and underneath the ball and use the other hand simply to hold the ball in place until ready to fire. As you start to push on upward with your shooting hand, drop your free hand away from the ball and let it swing out to your side for balance. Guide the ball off your fingertips, and follow through.

In the one-hand set shot some players hold the ball over their heads, sight under it at the basket, and release

Aiming the one-hand set shot . . . and releasing

the shot from the high position. It is a difficult shot to defend against. Although considered a less accurate form, the overhead one-hand set shot is often used effectively.

68

Free-throw. Most basketball players now favor the one-hand set shot when attempting a free throw. Its advantage is that you are able to use the same basic type of game shot that you have practiced a great deal. The difference between the free-throw and the one-hand set shot is that the free throw is always attempted from straight ahead and fifteen feet out from the basket, while the open-court set shot can be tried from any distance and from different angles.

Rarely will a player use a two-hand chest shot for free-throw attempts. On still rarer occasions, a player may resort to the old two-hand underhand free-throw method. The latter should be generally avoided. There is no other time or place on the court during a game for such a shot. So why waste your time practicing it? You could just as well be working on a shot that you can use most any place or any time.

Jump. Though effective, a one-hand set shot can sometimes be blocked by a clever, long-armed defenseman. In order to find a way around him—or, more accurately, a way *over* him—players began experimenting years ago with some kind of antigravity system by which they could get up above the defender's outstretched arms, pause for a moment, and release their shots. The best method they could find was simply to jump straight up in the air, hang there as long as gravity would allow, and launch the shot toward the basket before starting back down.

Thus, the jump shot was developed. First introduced on the West Coast, it quickly spread across the nation, and, indeed, the world. Today the jump shot is by far the most used shot in basketball. It is particularly effective for middle-distance shots from that area, ten to twenty feet from the basket, where peak action takes place.

Different players adapt the one-hand jump shot to their own styles. Usually, however, a jump shot begins with some deceptive move. For instance, you catch a pass a few yards out from the basket. A defender looms up in front of you, waving his arms and cutting off your opportunity to use a set shot or even sight on the basket. Still, he knows that you may jump, and he is prepared to jump with you. It's a one-on-one contest.

You square your shoulders to the basket and feint with your head, hoping he will think you're about to try going around him. You hope to trick him into moving first. Once he's committed, you can move in the opposite direction. You fake a jump, but your feet don't leave the floor. He bobs right up with you and bobs

Following some deceptive moves, feinting or faking, you can often get the jump on your defender, who has been caught floor-bound.

down again. You start to go through the motion again, and up he goes, sure that you're serious this time. But you stay planted for a split second. Your knees are still bent and ready to uncoil. Strung out and stretching up-

Usually you must shoot
over plenty of strong opposition.

ward, your opponent has jumped too soon. He's now
out of synchronization.

As he comes down, you take off. Springing high, you
bring the ball up over your head with both hands for
protection and control. As you hang momentarily in

midair at the peak of your leap, you sight on the basket and let your nonshooting hand drop away from the ball.

Nesting the ball in your upturned shooting hand, you snap your arm fully out and give a flip of your wrist to send the ball on its gentle trajectory toward the basket. As it rolls off your fingertips, you give it its final guidance correction with your index finger, the last finger in contact with the ball. And, as always, you follow

A driving jumper leaves the defenders
waving in empty air.

through toward the basket, to help add accuracy to your shot and also to draw a possible foul, which is part of the game.

The jump shot is basketball's most fearsome offensive weapon. It is difficult to master, but more difficult to defend against. To develop and perfect the shot, you must give it your most worthy effort.

Hook. The purpose of the hook shot is to get the ball headed toward the basket despite the heavy congestion around you. When you are faced by a determined defender, you drop your shoulder or feint with your head in order to get him to commit himself in one direction. Then, if his attention seems to be to the left and particularly if he moves in that direction, you pivot or step to the right (if you haven't already used up your allowable steps).

You start the ball from shoulder height, carrying it up with both hands. Then, as you sight over your left shoulder at the basket, take your supporting hand away from the ball. Do so by feel, for your eyes are on your target. You extend your shooting arm far out. You nest the ball in your fingers, somewhat like a round rock on the end of a catapult.

Now, with a smoothly looping motion, you hook the

ball over your head and toward the basket. As you do so, you are usually fading away from the basket and your defenders.

The hook shot is largely a matter of proper rhythm. Once you have it timed and set in motion, you must go through with it. If you have mastered its steps and practiced hard, you stand a good chance of making your two points.

A smoothly executed hook shot has balletlike overtones.

Work on the basic moves of these main shots. Fit in slight variations that suit your individual talents and style. As the basics become habit, and as more and more of your shots go through the hoop, you will be well on the way to earning a place on the team of your choice.

The three-second rule keeps the free-throw lane clear of loitering offensive players.

chapter five

CHOOSING A POSITION

Generally speaking, the five players on a basketball team do pretty much the same things. They dribble, pass, shoot, go after rebounds, and do anything else that is necessary to get possession of the ball and score a basket. The game is strictly a five-man effort, from the starting center tip to the final buzzer.

However, when choosing the position you want to play, certain factors can help you decide whether you should aim at becoming one of the two guards, one of the two forwards, or a center. (Players' responsibilities change quickly when a team suddenly gets the ball and switches from defense to offense. When explaining or diagramming plays, many coaches have started calling their defensive guards "quarterbacks" when they are on offense. Similarly, forwards on defense are called "wings," or "corners," when they switch to offense. The center, bent on batting down balls or grabbing rebounds around the key on defense, is called the "pivot man" on offense. He plays either high post, out near the foul line, or low post, as he works around and under the basket looking for a pass or taking a shot. So when a coach says that the right quarterback or pivot man does this or that, the guard or center knows the reference is to his duty when the team is on offense).

One can hardly deny that being tall has its advantages in basketball. And height is particularly important around the ten-foot-high basket. So, if you're not particularly tall, or, in fact, if you're a bit on the short side, you should consider playing guard.

To be a guard, you must do all things well. You must be a skillful ball handler, almost equally adept with either hand. You must also be a playmaker, able to guide the action of your team. As a guard, or quarterback, you must have lots of pep and hustle. You must keep your team's spirits up at all times, chattering and setting a good example. You must point out anything you might detect that will help your teammates take advantage of the opponents' weaknesses. You pretty much run the team, which is why on most teams the captain is a guard.

In the early days of all-court basketball, the duty of the guards was primarily to inbound the ball after the opponents had scored a basket, dribble upcourt and across the ten-second line, and pass the ball to the pivot man or to one of the forwards maneuvering in toward the basket. Then the guards would hang back near the center of the floor to protect against a fast break in case the ball fell into enemy hands. Guards were seldom high scorers. The few shots they took were usually from far out, tried only when the pivot man and forwards were bottled up.

Now the picture has changed. Of course, the guards are still charged with bringing the ball into the front court and also playing deep to protect against a fast break. They are still the main line of defense. But now

Despite the illegal elbow, this aggressive guard knows his job is to move the ball.

a guard may range all the way in to the basket. Often he will spot a clear path and drive for the basket to make a lay-up. He moves in and takes midrange jump shots. Sometimes he works his way into the corners, switching positions with a forward, who will cover for him outside in case the ball suddenly changes hands.

Playing guard has become such an all-court assignment that today guards take as many shots as anyone else on the team, sometimes more. However, many of a

This guard calls a play
as he brings the ball into the front court.

guard's shots will be taken at outside ranges of, say, eighteen to twenty-five feet. So, without neglecting the lay-ups and short shots, he must work particularly hard on the longer shots. Guards also usually lead the team in making assists, that is, getting possession of the ball and feeding it to a teammate for a shot.

If you're a good all-around player, though shorter than some, sure-fingered, speedy, spirited, and have the talents of a leader, then try out for one of the guard positions.

To be a forward, you don't really have to be tall, but it helps. By and large the two forwards are somewhat bigger men than the guards. Not always, of course, for in basketball, as in any other endeavor, skill and spirit are far more important than size. Still, height is an advantage the closer you play to the basket. Thus, the tallest players on a team are usually the forwards and, of course, the center.

As a forward, you must keep on the move at all times, whether or not you have the ball. In fact, moving around when you don't have the ball is as important as when you do. You must keep moving, trying to draw your opponent away from the line of fire so one of your teammates can get free and take a shot. Or you may set a screen to prevent an opponent from getting to your teammate with the ball. You must be in perpetual motion, weaving in around the basket, then back out to the corners. You must be a better than average outside shooter, for you will often try shots from the corners. But you must be particularly accurate from the middle distances of from ten to twenty feet. This territory is where jump shots are most effective, and as a forward you should work on the jump shots most. But you must also be able to execute lay-ups, hook shots, and others. Sometime during a game you will be called upon to use each of them.

A forward must be aggressive and a ball hawk. An extra inch or so of height will be to your advantage when you leap up through a sea of elbows, snag a rebound off the enemy backboard, and snap a clear-out pass to a teammate who is waiting to take it downcourt.

You must be able and willing to switch assignments smoothly with a guard who may suddenly have a "hot hand." You must be able to set a screen for him to shoot over. To screen a player merely means to maneuver yourself into a position between your teammate with the ball and the player who is guarding him. Thus the guard cannot reach him without barging into you, which is a foul. You must also be able to move out to protect the backcourt when your own guard moves in toward the basket for a shot.

The fact is that guards and forwards play pretty much the same game, except that they have primary responsibility for different areas of the court. Forwards stay in around the basket and the corners; the guards remain farther out.

To play center, however, you should be the tallest man on the team. You will make the center jumps, or tips, against the tallest man on the opposing team. On defense, you will guard the area around the foul lane,

After getting a rebound off the opponent's hoop, use a clear-out pass to get the ball headed quickly toward the far end of the court.

leaping and slapping down any shots that you can reach. You must, of course, slap them down while they are on the upward trajectory. If you interfere with a shot that is on its downward path to the hoop, you will be called for goaltending, and the shot will count whether or not it goes in.

As pivot man, you will handle the ball a great deal on offense. A guard may feed the ball to you somewhere around the key. Perhaps you can maneuver around the high post. Or you may prefer to drop back closer in under the basket to the low post. Even before the ball comes to you, you must know where the other players are and what they are doing. You pay particular attention to the forwards, who are weaving and dodging, trying to break into the clear. But you also may work a give-and-go with one of the guards. He slips you a quick pass, then breaks for the basket. You flip him a short return pass or hand the ball off to him as he streaks by. One dribble and he goes airborne for a lay-up.

As pivot man, you must keep moving in and out of the three-second zone, feeding the ball to your teammates maneuvering into shooting positions. Or you may reach out and take a pass, fake your opponent out of position, then whirl around for a hook shot, a lay-up, or whatever other short-range shot you have practiced. Most all of your shots will be made from less than fifteen feet out. That area—around the key—is the one on which you should concentrate.

More important than the position you play is your ability to "go both ways"—offense and defense. You must play the game to the hilt. When the ball unexpectedly changes hands, you must be able to switch

With the ball in its upward flight,
this position in defending the basket is legal.

quickly from offense to defense. You must play for all you're worth, regardless of whether your team has the ball and is driving for the basket or whether you are frantically falling back on defense in a desperate effort to stop your opponents' fast break.

Basketball takes all you've got, no matter what position you play.

In the low post, a pivot man whirls and takes a jump shot.

chapter six

OFFENSE

What you do with the basketball when your team has possession of it is offense. The main purpose of an offense is to put the basketball through the hoop. Doing so may sound simple, but five opposing players are dead set on preventing you.

An offense begins on any part of the court at the moment you get the ball. It continues until you or one of your teammates scores a basket, the basket is missed, a pass is stolen, someone is fouled, or your opponents suddenly take over the ball.

Then your offense suddenly becomes a defense, and every player on your team becomes a guard charged with halting the opponents' drive toward their own basket.

During an offensive charge down the floor, only one man at a time, of course, can have actual possession of the ball. Therefore, about ninety percent of the time a player must move empty-handed, although with just as much purpose as a player getting ready to pass or setting up to take a shot. The primary purpose of your movements should be to draw your defender away from the play and to open up the court for your teammate with the ball. At the same time you should maneuver into a position where you can reach out for a pass, go in to take a rebound off the boards, or be ready to set up a rearguard action in case there's a turnover and the ball suddenly changes hands.

Above all, keep moving. Always keep moving.

When working the ball downcourt toward your basket, you should avoid dribbling if possible. Passes are

Keep moving to draw your defenders out of position
to give a teammate a chance to shoot.

faster and are usually the best method for moving the ball around between players. Try to keep your passes going in a forward direction toward your basket. A cross-court pass is easy to intercept, and whoever steals such a pass usually has a good head start toward his own basket.

Three or four well-directed passes can move the ball the full length of the court, without once touching the hardwood, and end up in a lay-up shot. In the case of a professional game, where such action is allowed, a series of passes may end up with a slam dunk, or stuff shot. A slam dunk occurs when a tall player with the ball leaps up and stuffs the ball down through the hoop. But this shot is rarely legal in school play, where the ball must be released outside the cone of the basket, so is best forgotten—unless or until you become a pro.

Despite the importance of passing, there are times when dribbling is effective. While forwards and the center rush to their positions at the basket end of the court, one of the guards can dribble the ball up court, cross the center dividing line, and prepare to set up a play.

Dribbling slowly into the front court, the guard calls a play or holds up some fingers to signal the action he wants. The play begins as all contestants start to weave,

A dunk, or stuff shot, is legal in professional basketball,
but illegal in high-school and most college play.

pass, and pivot in a practiced pattern. The players must
take care to keep the play spread out and not bunch up
under the basket.

You are a forward, and soon one of your teammates
sets a screen for you. Before the defender can move
around the screen to get at you, you take a pass, square
your shoulders to the basket, and flip a ten-foot jump

90

shot through the hoop. Or you may run a pick, meaning that you maneuver with the ball so that if your guard tries to stay with you, he will collide with one of your teammates. As he slows down to avoid such a charging foul, you take a shot or drive on in toward the basket.

The next time the team gets the ball, it attacks down

Try to get inside of your guard
to get a clear shot at the basket.

the opposite side of the court. To be effective, the players must mix up their offensive strategies so the opponents will not be able to perfect their defense.

Sometimes the team uses a fast break to catch the defense back on its heels. On fast breaks there is no time to call any particular strategy. Having played together for so long, each teammate knows what he should do and how to do it. Everyone keeps moving, with or without the ball. The players work their patterns automatically. Their whole concern is to get the ball downcourt and into the basket as quickly as possible. Dribbling is used only when the team can't pass. Dribbling, being slower than passing, actually helps the opponents set their defense.

A good offense will have a catalog of set plays to be used in specific situations. Some teams go in heavily for such planned offenses. Other teams leave the offensive maneuvers pretty much up to the practiced experience of the players, their aggressiveness, and desire to win. Something is to be said for both methods. The ideal is to have at least a few set plays for special occasions. For instance, a team needs an established play to use when inbounding a ball against the opponents' defensive setup. Or it needs one or more set plays to work off a center tip or a toss-up at the foul line. Probably it will have a few plays to work off the pivot man, passing the ball back and forth until someone gets free under the basket. Once in a while, with a prepracticed play, a team can crowd one side of the court, clearing a corner for a good jump shooter to take a shot.

Also a controlled game, in which the ball is usually worked according to a practiced plan, has the advantage of fewer errors and mix-ups. Players know pretty much what to expect and have time to prepare.

Get inside and spread out in order to block your opponents and grab a rebound.

Whether using planned plays or running an offense "by ear," each player must stay with the fundamentals of running, passing, dribbling, faking, and shooting. But he should be able to use them in whatever manner will match the moment and get the ball to the basket.

Although the function of the offense is to score points, a team must move the ball deliberately in order to get close enough to the basket to take only high-percentage shots. Unless you, one of the forwards, are in a fast-break situation, don't rush things. Set a pace that will give everyone time to reach his proper position. Of course, speed is usually an advantage. If you can set a pace sufficient to outdistance your opponents, you can work the ball close in to the basket before they set up their barricade of blocking bodies and reaching arms.

Still, don't hurry your shots. When you're guarded, or the possibility of getting off a clean shot is slim, pass off to a teammate. The assist is often as important as the shot. If he can't shoot, you can set up and try again.

The offense is not charged with the single function of working the ball downcourt and taking shots at the basket. Its other important objective is to keep possession of the ball. Only through possession can the team hope to score. So if a pass goes awry, you must scramble to recover the ball before an opposing player grabs it. If you can't get full possession, at least you can try to tie it up so there will be a jump ball.

One of the most important functions you have is to get offensive rebounds off the backboard. Any time a shot is missed, and the ball ricochets off the rim or the backboard, it is a free ball. If a player on the opposing team manages to leap up and get it, you switch roles from offense to defense immediately, and the game does an about-face.

If, however, you are able to outmaneuver the defense and take the rebound yourself, your team still has the ball, and you are still on offense. Being there close to your own basket, you have an excellent opportunity to take another shot or to pass out to a teammate, who may set up another play. The importance of rebounding cannot be overstressed. A good rebounding team wins many a game that might otherwise be a toss-up.

There are a few tricks to good offensive rebounding. Chances are that a misfired ball will go beyond the basket, since its momentum carries it that way. When the shot is on its way, your opponent usually quits guarding you. He turns his attention to the basket, intent upon the rebound. Now is your chance to drive toward the spot beyond the goal to which you believe the ball is most likely to ricochet. If it doesn't rebound in your direction, you can often pull up or change course and still have a try at it. A great deal of rebounding skill lies in correct anticipation.

When rebounding, always try to establish the inside position before your opponents get a chance. Spread your legs, get your hands up high, and block your opponents' access to the basket. Thrust your rump subtley

A rebounder often gets a chance for a second shot.

into him, or otherwise try to maintain body contact in order to keep him behind you and know what he is doing. When you and a teammate work together, you can form quite a barrier in front of the basket and be in position to get a majority of rebounds.

When rebounding, if you are unable to get a firm grip on the ball or aren't in a position from which you can attempt a tip-in through the basket, tap the ball back to one of the guards near the top of the key. Clearing the ball out this way maintains possession and allows your team another offensive thrust at the basket.

Since keeping possession of the ball is so important to any offense, you must avoid violations of play, at which point the ball is turned over to the other team. For instance, don't be careless in dribbling. If you stop your dribble, then start again, it's a double dribble. You must not get your hand under a ball and carry it over during a high dribble, or you will be called for palming. Big-handed pros sometimes grip the ball during a dribble, which also is palming and another turnover to the opposition. Moving your pivot foot or taking more than the allowed one-two rhythm steps before stopping or getting rid of the ball is traveling.

If you fail to get the ball across the center line within

ten seconds, you violate a rule. Once across the line, you must stay across it as long as your team keeps possession of the ball. You break rules also if you deliberately kick the ball or strike it with a closed fist. Staying more than three seconds at a time in the key is another infraction.

If you are guilty of any of these violations—and there are others—your team loses possession of the ball. Since, without the ball you have no chance to score, you must pay strict attention to the rules of the game.

In essence, an effective offense is made up of five players, each busily doing his part to the best of his ability. Remember, a workable offense always depends upon a player's being able to fit his part into the efforts of his teammates.

There are no individual players in basketball. Only team players.

Your team can have the best shots of any basket-ballers around. But unless you and your teammates can prevent the opposing players from scoring even one more point than you do, you will not win games.

Team defense means keeping the other team from making easy baskets. There are no shutouts in basketball, no scoreless games. A team is bound to score on you. But if you allow them to score easily, you're sure to lose. Obviously defense is as important to a team as offense, and often it is considered more so.

There are two basic types of defense—man-to-man and zone. On man-to-man defense you have one particular player to guard. You stick with him step for step whenever his team has the ball and wherever he may go. Without actually tying him down and sitting on him, you hound your man, talk to him, harass him, try to upset his rhythm, and, in every way legally possible, prevent him from handling the ball with any degree of skill.

On zone defense you are charged with protecting a particular area of the basketball court in the general vicinity of the basket. You guard whoever enters into your zone, usually staying between him and the basket. When each defending player keeps a close guard over his zone, the opponents are forced to take long, low-percentage shots.

Regardless of whether you play man-to-man or zone, what you really play is team defense. Each player fulfills his particular assignment while helping the others prevent the opponents from dribbling, passing, or getting in close to the basket for a high-percentage shot. You must keep pressure on your man, so he will hurry

Man-to-man defense primarily puts you against a single opponent.

Any defense is charged with keeping pressure
on the ball handler.

his passes or his shots and make errors. After all, the
prime duty of the defense is to force errors and get the
ball back.

You may need to take calculated risks and try to get
the ball, in addition to guarding your man. Attempt to

bat it down. Try to steal it, but only if you can do so without getting yourself out of defensive position.

When confronting an opponent straight on, keep your eyes on his chest, not on his eyes or head. He can fake with his eyes or feint with his head and sucker you into a premature move. But where his chest goes, he must go, too. Make him move first, then react.

If you can keep him uncertain and a bit off-balance, you may get the chance to reach out and hook the ball away from him. Just be careful you don't hit him and foul him while you're going for the ball.

Don't hesitate to use your voice to distract him and upset his concentration. The idea of the defense is to befuddle the opposition so that it can't function effectively. It's all fair.

In a man-to-man defense, when the player you are guarding does not have the ball, you can sag off a little on your coverage of him. Even while staying between him and the basket, you may still have the opportunity to slide over and lend a little double-teaming support to a teammate who is guarding a player in a more dangerous position to shoot. Talk to your teammates so you will know what to expect of each other.

Only you can determine when double-teaming is safe.

Opposite, top: In keeping a position between your man and the basket, you also defend against a pass.
Bottom: Be prepared to defend against high and low balls.

You must never let the man you are supposed to guard get free enough to make a break for the basket or get into a favorable position to receive a pass. Sometimes trying to figure where your support is most needed is like trying to pat your head and rub your stomach at the same time. But a defenseman who can vary his coverage and help a teammate is valuable.

At times things become congested, and you find yourself cut off or screened from the man you are supposed to be guarding. Size up the situation and quickly call "Help!" For the time being you may trade responsibilities with a teammate, covering his man, as he calls "Switch," and covers yours. As soon as things settle down, each of you gets back to your regular opponent.

Since your main job of defense is to keep your man from scoring, your best bet is to stay in front of him. Guard him from a distance of about three feet. Stay close enough to keep him from shooting, passing, or dribbling, but not so close as to allow him to fake and go around you.

Set yourself to block his path. Stand with your feet comfortably apart. Keep your elbows in. Thrust one arm out low to knock down bounce passes or perhaps steal the ball. This stance also discourages your opponent from trying to dribble or dodge past you. Keep your other hand up and waving in his face to disconcert him or bat down an attempted overhead pass or shot.

Maintain your balance at all times. Be ready to move in any direction. He undoubtedly will try to fake you out and move the opposite way. If you have studied his habits, as you should, you may know what to expect. Correct anticipation is half the job of a good defense.

When he moves, you move with him. Avoid using crossover steps when possible as you may get entangled

Be careful not to let your man feint you out and go around you.

in your own feet. Use sliding steps. Shuffle your forward foot in the direction you want to go, follow with your trailing foot and shuffle again. The movement is similar to a prizefighter's sliding steps across the canvas of the ring. With a little practice you will be amazed at how quickly you can move with your man in this manner.

Sliding steps work just as well if you're going backward. You simply start with your rear foot and follow with your front foot. Over and over, you can go straight back or at an angle that will crowd your man toward

In defending against a dribbler,
try to crowd him toward the sideline.

the sideline. Always try to make him move to the outside, thus closing off any inward avenues he may have to the basket.

However, you mustn't rely on using sliding steps only. Remember, your most important duty is to keep your position on your opponent. Stay between him and the basket, and prevent him from getting around you, passing, or shooting. If you can't stay with him by using sliding steps, use whatever type of running is called for to accomplish your job.

Never leave any doubt about which man you are going to cover. Once you get back to your position on defense, and your man arrives, point to him so your teammates will know he's yours. Then you take him on, sticking with him, using brisk steps, keeping between him and the basket.

Although your primary attention is on the man you are guarding, you must always be aware of where the ball is. Sometimes a quick sliding step—not enough to free your man from coverage—will get you into position to intercept a pass or block the path of a dribbler.

Another of your big jobs on defense is to vie with the offensive players to recover rebounds. Here you have a slight advantage, for if you are playing your position

In guarding your opponent, use sliding steps when possible.

correctly you have maneuvered in between your man and the basket when the shot is taken. Thus, being closer to the basket, you are in good position to block out your man. To do so, as soon as the shot is on its way, turn toward the basket. Spread-eagle yourself, legs well apart and hands up. Waiting thus, six or so feet out from under the basket, you form a formidable barrier that

Scrambling for a rebound off the backboard

your opponent will have a tough time penetrating without fouling you.

In setting your position for a rebound, don't get so close in under the basket that the ball can go over your head if it ricochets. Reach up and try to grab the rebound with both hands if possible. Get possession of it. Bring it down close to your chin for protection. Then pass the ball out quickly to a teammate along the sideline in order to get the action going in the opposite direction. This play is called an "outlet" pass.

If you are unable to get hold of the ball, you may swat it. Try anything, to keep it from falling into enemy hands. Just be sure to swat it far out away from the basket, hoping one of your teammates will get it. If not, at least you have sent it out of the critical danger zone near the basket.

One of the more fearsome forms of defense is the full-court press. With this tactic, you don't wait for your opponents to bring the ball over the center line before you start guarding them. You glue yourself to your man from the moment the ball is put in play anywhere on the court. The constant harassment often so unnerves a team that it is unable to get the ball over the center line within the ten-second time limit. Then the opponents get possession of the ball.

At the very least, a full-court press tends to upset whatever plans your opponents may have. There is always the risk, of course, that some player will break loose and head for the sparsely guarded basket for an easy lay-up. So in a pressing defense you must not let your man get closer to the basket than you are.

110

A full-court press is also a tiring tactic, demanding more running than usual. But it is equally as hard on opponents. Whichever team is in better physical condition usually gains an advantage from it.

If a team is playing a zone defense, each player concentrates on whoever invades his territory, not on any specific opponent. A zone defense is seldom as aggressive as a man-to-man defense. Nor is it as lively or interesting to watch, which is one reason why the zone defense is not used in professional basketball where paying customers prefer man-to-man action. Although zone defenses are still used in some schools, most teams that win consistently rely on each player sticking to his one man and making his life so generally miserable out on the floor that he is unable to pass, catch, dribble, or shoot the ball.

Many teams also play a combination defense, incorporating parts of both man-to-man and zone defenses.

Yet, with all the guarding and all the ball hawking on defense, there are certain hazards. In your eagerness you are apt to commit violations of rules or fouls. Fouls, particularly personal fouls committed by one player against another, are costly. Although they are seldom deliberate, officials may be quick to blow their whistles, giving the offended player one or more free throws. Many basketball games are won by a slim margin of points, so handing free throws to your opponents is like giving your cat a key to the canary cage.

So play hard, but avoid such fouls as holding. You cannot grasp a player by his uniform or any part of his body in an attempt to slow his progress. Nor can you shove a player without being called for pushing.

Barging into a player who is standing still, or who has the so-called right-of-way to a path of travel, is considered charging, still another common foul.

Making contact from the rear, such as trying to reach over an opponent's shoulder to grab a rebound off the backboard, is a foul. So is tripping, sticking a knee out in a player's path, or warding off an opponent with an excessive use of your elbows. When trying to knock the ball away from a player, if you hit his forearm or wrist, you will be called for hacking.

For the first few common fouls of each quarter or half (a number that varies in school and pro games) the opponents get the ball out-of-bounds. However, the victims of fouls in excess of that number are awarded free throws. Usually this penalty is one-and-one. If he makes the first free throw, the player gets the chance for a second or bonus shot. Thus, he can score up to two points. But if he misses the first try, the ball is in play, and he doesn't get a second shot.

If you commit your foul while the player is in the act of shooting, he is awarded two free throws. (In pro basketball there is an additional rule for free throws. If your team has gone over the limit of personal fouls in a period, a player fouled in the act of shooting has three shots to score his two points. If he makes the first two shots, he does not take a third shot.)

Left: Guarding too close from the rear is a foul.
Right: This is a holding foul.

Five personal fouls (six in professional play) put you out of the game.

So, as you see, fouls are costly and, despite the heat of competition, should be carefully avoided.

A challenging defense is usually a game-winning defense. You play it both by plan and by ear, adjusting to the threat of each offensive situation. As the ball gets worked in closer to the basket you must tighten up. Set yourself as a moving barrier between your man and the basket. But don't be discouraged if your opponents happen to score. Your job is not to shut them out—after all, every team scores—but to guard and pester them and reduce their shooting percentage.

Communicate with your teammates. Talk things up. Shout "Got it!" if suddenly you come up with a rebound. Then your teammates can quickly shift into offensive action.

During quiet moments of the game, or during time out, talk things over with your teammates. Point out weaknesses in the opponents' offense or defense and suggest ways in which you can take advantage of them. Keep team spirits up.

A team that scores well may get most of the cheers. But a team that defends well wins most of the games.

chapter eight
HIT THE HOOP

It's the big game. Packed bleachers. A buzzer ends the warm-up period.

You and your teammates form a circle in front of the players' bench. While the crowd cheers behind you, you stack hands together in a team clasp. There are sweaty hands, cold hands, calm hands, and shaky hands. But all are eager hands.

Then, as each name echoes from the public-address speakers, one at a time you leap out onto the court, shouting and gesticulating with fierce fists and victory signs. Spirits are high. You take your guard position, eagerly waiting for action to begin.

A whistle shrills, then the center tip, and the game is under way.

The first half is a ding-dong battle, with the lead changing hands a half-dozen times. Everyone uses those carefully learned fundamentals to good advantage. Crisp passing. Careful dribbling. Shooting only the good percentage shots from close in.

Then your opponents tighten their defense. You have

A center tip—and the game is under way.

to start shooting from farther out. The shots miss. The opponents get the rebounds and start on their own campaign of baskets, dropping them in at regular intervals.

The half ends 29-22. You're on the short end. Disaster.

During intermission the coach pleads, "Defense, fellows. Defense! Play the boards. You're letting them get the ball. They're taking too many shots."

So you go out in the third quarter determined to keep

them away from the basket. It's not that easy. They're good.

Then, suddenly from out of the blue, you get a "hot hand." Swish . . . swish . . . swish. The ball has "eyes!" Seven out of nine field-goal attempts, plus two free throws for a spectacular sixteen points. At the end of the third quarter you have a comfortable eight-point lead.

But, early in the final quarter, you lose that magic touch, for no reason that you can figure. You keep doing the same things the same way—fake, feint, eyes on target. Jump, hang in midair, release the ball carefully off

You work the ball toward the basket.

your fingertips . . . and watch it twang off the rim. Six straight misses.

And now, in the final few seconds of the game, your team is in deep trouble. You are on the short end of a 62-61 score. You are on the verge of losing the championship toward which you have worked all season. It may be decided by a single lousy point.

You wonder why the coach doesn't bench you. But you are glad he doesn't, and you keep playing your heart out. You notice, however, that your teammates don't feed you the ball as regularly as they did when you were hitting. Who can blame them?

Suddenly you're in a nine-second clutch. Nine seconds until the final buzzer. Nine seconds spelling victory or defeat. Your last chance.

You dribble quickly across the center line. You see the forwards dodge around trying to shake their defenders, trying to maneuver into place to take a pass and get off a shot. There is desperation in their eyes. Now less than seven seconds remain.

Your pivot man pulls up in the high post near the free-throw line, just outside the three-second lane. He turns toward you, holding his hands ready to receive a pass. He is crowded closely from behind by his defender. Your running mate, the other guard, heads down the sideline, cuts toward the basket, and continues on around. He is dogged every foot of the way by his determined guard.

Five seconds.

"Shoot!" A wave of sound comes from the stands. "Shoot!"

You are tempted. But your guard looms in front of you, reaching high, waving his arms in your face, shouting to distract you. You fake a leap. He doesn't fall for it. You feint to the right with your shoulders. He leans with you, but only a little, as he struggles for balance. He wants to be ready to move only if you move.

Yet, as he leans, a small opening appears on the left side. You don't hesitate. You can't afford to. Three seconds!

You duck under the guard's outstretched arm, bend low to the left, and snap a bounce pass to the pivot man. You don't wait to see whether or not he gets off the shot. You cut around your defender and follow the ball.

The pivot man sees you coming. He knows what you have in mind. You can see a hopeful grin appear on his face as he takes a single step, which blocks his defender from shifting over into your path.

Then, as you race past, the center flips a short pass to you. It's high enough so that you don't have to bend to catch it. It's high enough so that you take it in midleap toward the basket. So far it's as neat a give-and-go play as you have worked all season.

All that's left is the lay-up. You can't miss. Or can you? Many a cinch lay-up, in many a critical moment, has somehow spun mysteriously off the rim.

So, while in midair, you sight carefully at the so-called sweet spot on the backboard. Quite gently, with just enough momentum to give it the proper bounce, you lay the ball against the surface—and watch it bank cleanly down through the hoop.

You don't hear the final buzzer through the explosion of sound that rocks the auditorium. You're only slightly aware of friendly hands mauling you. All you know is that you feel great . . . really great. It was some game.

A wonderful game!

Assist—a pass to a teammate who scores.

Backboard—the board on which the hoop is hung.

Backcourt—the half of the court that contains the opponent's basket.

Ball hawk—a player who scrambles and recovers loose balls.

Base line—*see* End line.

Basket—the metal ring, eighteen inches in diameter, attached to the backboard ten feet from the floor on which the net is suspended.

Block—to impede, by contact, an opponent who doesn't have the ball.

Bonus shot—an additional free-throw attempt sometimes awarded if the first shot is successful.

Bounce pass—a pass that is bounced to the receiver.

Center jump—*see* Jump ball.

Center line—*see* Division line.

Center tip—*see* Jump ball.

Charging—personal contact with an opponent who is standing still; a foul.

Defense—the team not in possession of the ball.

Division line—the line that divides the basketball court in half.

Double dribble—a violation occurring when the player interrupts his dribble, then starts again.

Double team—two defensive players guarding one offensive player.

Dribble—to move the ball by bouncing or batting it to the floor and retaining possession.

End line—the end boundary line of the court.

Fast break—a maneuver in which the offense rushes the ball down-court into scoring position before the defense can get set.

Foul—an infraction of the game rules; also to commit an infraction.

Foul circle—the semicircle at the outer end of the free-throw lane.

Foul lane—*see* Free-throw lane.

Foul line—*see* Free-throw line.

Free-throw shot—an unimpeded shot from behind the free-throw line.

Free-throw circle—*see* Foul circle.

Free-throw lane—the rectangular area and semicircle from the end line to the free-throw line.

Free-throw line—a line fifteen feet from the backboard, from which penalty shots are attempted.

Front court—the area between the division line and a team's basket.

Full-court press—a tactic in which a team defends in the back-court as well as in the front court; can use both zone and man-to-man strategy.

Give-and-go—to pass to a teammate, then take a short return pass from him while cutting for the basket.

Goal—score made when the ball passes through the basket; also an object or area toward which the ball is advanced.

Goaltending—touching the ball or basket while the ball is on, above, or within the opponent's basket, or on downward flight toward the basket.

Guard—to defend against an opponent.

Hacking—to chop down on a player's wrists or forearms as he attempts to shoot.

Held ball—occurs when two opponents grasp the ball simultaneously, or when the player with the ball is so closely guarded that he is unable to dribble or pass within five seconds; results in a jump ball.

122

High post—offensive area near the free-throw circle.

Holding—grasping an opponent by the uniform or any part of his body.

Hoop—*see* Basket.

Jump ball—method of putting the ball into play by referee who tosses it up between two opponents at the center jump circle or either of the foul circles.

Key—the free-throw lane and foul circle.

Lead pass—a pass thrown ahead of player so that he has to catch up with the ball.

Long-shot zone—in ABA competition, a twenty-five-foot zone around the basket; a shot made from outside the zone counts three points.

Loose-ball foul—a foul committed during the time neither team is in possession of the ball.

Low post—offensive area outside the key but close in to the basket.

Man-to-man defense—a method of defense in which each player guards an assigned member of the offensive team.

Net—the cone of cording attached to the basket ring.

Offense—the team in possession of the ball.

Out-of-bounds—the ball or the player is outside the end line or sideline.

Overtime—extra period(s) of time used to decide a game that ends in a tie during regulation play.

Palming—to grasp the ball while dribbling or to get your palm beneath it and carry it over.

Pick—a maneuver for cutting off an opponent from play.

Pivot—while holding the ball, the action of stepping any number of times with the same foot, but maintaining the other foot (pivot foot) at its point of contact with the floor; also man playing the center position on offense.

Playmaker—the player, usually a guard, who calls play signals; sometimes called "quarterback," as in football.

Rebound—a ball that bounces off the basket or backboard after an unsuccessful shot.

Screen—to block an opponent without making actual contact.

Slam dunk—a shot in which the ball is slammed down through the basket from above the rim; illegal in high-school and most college play.

Stuff shot—*see* Slam dunk.

Switch—to change guarding assignments.

Three-point play—an extra free-throw attempt awarded to a player who is fouled while scoring a basket.

Throw-in—to put the ball in play from out-of-bounds.

Ten-second line—*see* Division line.

Tip-in—tapping in the rebound of a missed shot.

Traveling—to run with the ball or to move your pivot foot.

Turnover—loss of ball possession without a shot being taken.

Violation—generally an infraction of game rules less serious than a foul and usually involving play technicalities.

Wing man—an offensive player, normally a forward, working the corners of the front court.

Zone defense—a method of defense in which players cover assigned areas rather than specific opponents.

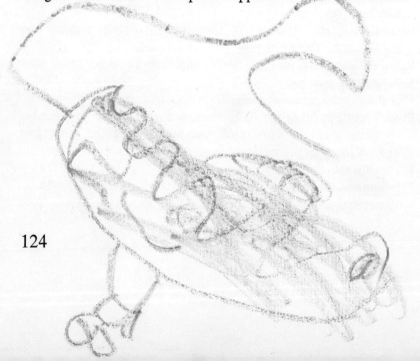

indicates illustration

Charles (Chick) Coombs graduated from the University of California at Los Angeles and decided at once to make writing his career. While working at a variety of jobs, he labored at his typewriter early in the morning and late at night. An athlete at school and college, Mr. Coombs began by writing sports fiction. He soon broadened his interests, writing adventure and mystery stories, and factual articles as well. When he had sold over a hundred stories, he decided to try one year of full-time writing, chiefly for young people, and the results justified the decision.

Eventually he turned to writing books. To date he has published more than sixty books, both fiction and nonfiction, covering a wide range of subjects, from aviation and space, to oceanography, drag racing, motorcycling, and many others. He is also author of the Be a Winner series of books explaining how various sports are played and how to succeed in them.

Mr. Coombs and his wife Eleanor live in Westlake Village, near Los Angeles.

LAMBS ELEMENTARY SCHOOL

LAMBS ELEMENTARY SCHOOL

LAMBS ELEMENTARY SCHOOL